Praise for Pastiche

In detailing a range of experiences in her life, Marjorie Pagel helps us see how and why the daily chores, struggles, and joys she once thought commonplace, she now regards "with reverence." With her as guide, I found myself growing not only in appreciation of her sense of adventure, but also in appreciation of the "everyday miracles" of my own life.

—Margaret Rozga, Wisconsin Poet Laureate, 2019-2020, and author of five full-length poetry collections, most recently, *Restoring Prairie.*

What strikes me about the whole collection is its undercurrents of optimism and possibility. If one can endure the slings and arrows throughout a long life and still have those qualities, well, it's amazing. And they produce something worth reading.

—Nancy Backes, PhD, English professor and theater dramaturg

In this new collection of tightly crafted, intimate, and poignant prose and poetry, Marjorie Pagel unpacks moments from her own life that reveal greater truths about family, relationships, and resilience. These gentle insights into her own and her family's challenges inspire understanding and joy.

> —Bruce H. Campbell, MD, author of *A Fullness of Uncertain Significance: Stories of Surgery, Clarity, and Grace*

Marjorie Pagel's beautifully-written collection of insights, images, and striking moments of spirituality comes as a welcome gift to all of us who are seeking respite from the world's prevailing despair.

> —Marilyn L. Taylor, Wisconsin Poet Laureate, 2009-2010

At a time when it seems all our heroes must be super, Marjorie Pagel finds the heroic in an ordinary life.

> —Jennifer Rupp writes historical fiction under the pen name, Jennifer Trethewey, translating her love for Scotland into her series of historical romance novels, the Highlanders of Balforss, featuring brawny Scots, sweeping romance, and non-stop adventure, all laced with a liberal dose of humor.

In her new Pastiche, a collection of poems and prose, Marjorie Pagel is at her best — wisely and gently, but also humorously, taking the commonplace and, in her words, regarding it with reverence.

—Ronnie Hess is a poet who has served on the Boards of the Wisconsin Fellowship of Poets, the Friends of Lorine Niedecker, and the Wisconsin Poet Laureate Commission.

By turns poignant and revealing, Marjorie Pagel's Pastiche: A Memoir in Poetry and Prose offers glimpses into the author's rich and varied life in Wisconsin. With charming black and white illustrations, Pastiche is a rewarding read. One observation sums it up: "You know what it is to cherish what you have, to enjoy each moment as it comes." A final poem, "When I Die," sums it up in a similar way: "Just a sweet savoring of the minutes at hand."

—Ed Block is Emeritus Professor of English at Marquette University, Milwaukee, WI. His most recent collection of poems, *Banners of Longing,* appeared in 2024.

As I read the stories in this collection, I kept looking up expecting to see Marjorie herself sitting across from me, asking if I'd like a little more coffee, then taking a breath before breaking into another story. Yes to more coffee, I'd say, and yes to more stories because you can't read just one without wanting to hear more. Told in a tell it like it is, matter of fact voice, Marjorie parts the curtain, allowing us to experience the world and the people she has come from, and what she has learned along the way. This is sound storytelling from a writer who doesn't miss a thing.

Marjorie Pagel's Pastiche is packed full of wisdom. Through these essays and poems, Pagel has dug deep and found rich insights and hard-won joy. Pagel's ability to reflect on her experiences inspires me to grab my own journal. Readers who've tried to make sense of their growing up years as well as the changes and chances of life will find a kindred spirit in these pages.

With Pastiche, Marjorie Pagel once again offers her readers a collection of sensitive and deeply introspective prose and poetry written with her characteristic unflinching honesty and in her refreshingly unembellished style.

Also by Marjorie Pagel

The Romance of Anna Smith and Other Stories

Where I'm From: Poems and Stories

Pastiche

A memoir in poetry and prose

Marjorie Pagel

Hidden Timber Books

MILWAUKEE, WISCONSIN

Marjorie Pagel/Hidden Timber Books
6650 West State Street, #D98
Milwaukee, WI 53213
hiddentimberbooks.com

Cover artwork: Matthew Pasersky
Interior art (dedication page and pages 12, 14, 31, 59): Jean Berens
Additional artwork by Ekaterina and Elizaveta

Pastiche: A memoir in poetry and prose/Marjorie Pagel.
-- 1st ed.
ISBN 979-8-9873517-1-0

To my grandchildren:
Matthew, Ella, and Graham Pasersky

Contents

To the Reader..i

Remnants..1

Looking for My Muse...................................5

Wonder Woman in the Shower 7

In Jean's Garden 9

Auntie Ruth's Suitcase......................... 13

Do We Measure Up? 17

Social Distancing: a farm wife's story................23

Stones: a story of two retreats 27

Whatever Happened to the Baby in the John?...33

Not All Those Who Wander Are Lost..................39

It's In Our Blood, You Know 43

No Uncommon Thing.......................................49

Wherever You Go, There You Are 53

Around the Campfire......................................59

Glad to be Alive 65

Family Secrets..................................... 69

Enough 73

Dear Mrs. Griggs 75

When I Die 81

Acknowledgements 84

About the Author 86

Travels with My Muse 88

To the Reader

Over the past forty years I've been a regular participant in numerous writers' groups, notably those offered by Redbird Studios (Judy Bridges), Red Oak Writing (Kim Suhr), and Pen to Paper (Christi Craig). Most of the poems and short prose pieces included in this chapbook have been read by other writers in those groups. I was especially encouraged two decades ago by Jeannée Sacken, who was leading one of the roundtable critique groups, when she looked at me with clear, penetrating eyes and implored, "Tell us more." It was precisely the encouragement I needed.

In those days I had started a practice inspired by Julia Cameron's Morning Pages. I called my unedited ramblings MP's MPs (for Marjorie Pagel's Morning Pages) and often polished them up a bit for roundtable. Everyone seemed to enjoy my creative writing exercises; Carol Wobig and Jennifer Rupp told me how much they'd like to spend some time traveling along with the thoughts buzzing around inside my head. I don't know what I relished more – entertaining writers at the roundtable or giving myself free rein to entertain my own thoughts, following them wherever they would take me.

One of my favorite authors, Fredrik Backman, dedicated his novel *Anxious People*: "To the voices in my head, the most remarkable of my friends. And to my wife, who lives with us."

I know exactly what he means.

Remnants

When my mother died, she left behind a storage room filled with fabric. Mostly "remnants," as she called the bits and pieces of broadcloth, denim, gingham, and corduroy that had accumulated over her lifetime, but there were some larger pieces as well – enough to make a child's dress, a woman's skirt. Certainly enough to keep an active quiltmaker busy for years.

My two sisters and I sorted through Mom's remnants, stopping to remember the little girl's pinafore or bridesmaid's gown that had been fashioned from the very same material we held in our hands. We all took a few choice pieces of fabric for ourselves – for our own "someday" projects – leaving the rest for Goodwill.

Our mother was a competent seamstress. When I was six years old and a flower girl in my Aunt Maisie's wedding, she made me a long-length white satin dress to match the bride's gown. Years later she sewed my sister Wanda's bridal gown, and for my own wedding she made bridesmaids' dresses for both my sisters as well as the flower girls' dresses for my nieces, Cheryl and Kendra. Over the years, there were checked gingham dresses with smocking for her granddaughters, and countless projects, including alterations and mending for friends, relatives, and neighbors.

With our mother's guidance, all three of us girls – her daughters – learned to sew. The machine I learned on was a Singer treadle, though by the time I got to high school, Mom had an electric model. I clearly remember her rolling out a bolt of fabric on the kitchen table, affixing tissue paper pattern pieces with straight pins, then cutting along the dark lines of the pattern.

Every sewing project resulted in bits and pieces of leftover fabric: the "remnants" I mentioned above. Mom used some of these remnants for doll clothes or patchwork quilts. The rest were piled in that small storage room off the upstairs hallway.

I thought of my mother and her closet full of remnants when I visited a quilt exhibit at the Milwaukee Art Museum. These quilts weren't made of geometric blocks in the usual patchwork pattern. They were fashioned together from whatever bits and pieces of fabric the women from Gee's Bend, Alabama, could find.

The African American women from this poverty-stricken area learned to improvise, stitching many tiny, asymmetrical strips of fabric together. They didn't have the luxury of following a particular color scheme. And yet all of these finished quilts were artistic masterpieces in their own right.

Gee's Bend women began making bedcovers from strips of cloth after the Civil War and into the 20th century. These quilts kept the women and their children warm inside the unheated shacks where they lived without running water or electricity. Like uncounted numbers of women from all times and places, they learned to create beauty from what materials were available to them. They were practical, they were recyclers, they were artists.

The stories of the women who made the quilts came along with the exhibit, and as I stood in admiration before each particular work of art, listening to the audio of the artist speaking, I remained transfixed before their photographic images, moved almost to tears.

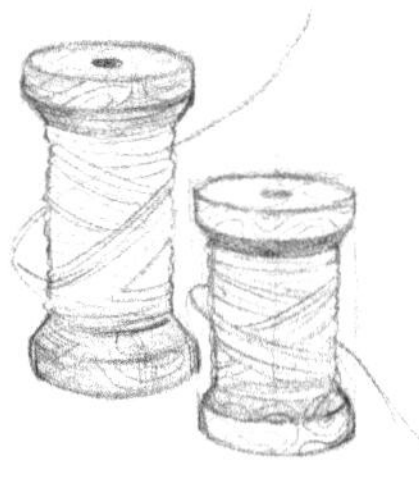

When anyone dies there are remnants of one kind or another left behind. Some of these we dispense with, others we bring into our own homes. The other kind of remnants – our memories – remain as well. As I grow older, I find myself carrying these bits and pieces with me – these remnants of other lives, other days.

Looking for
My Muse

I'd like a traveling kind of muse –
one that goes everywhere with me
sees everything the way a poet needs to
with wonder and delight.
Dismay sometimes too, and anguish,
calling me to be a voice for social justice,
world peace, human kindness.
I'd like a muse like that.

I need a muse that doesn't miss a trick
sees into darkened corners, nudges
those almost invisible nuggets
from their hiding places.
My muse should be strict,
like my old Sunday school teacher –
dismissing my excuses
prodding my reluctance

bolstering my self-confidence.
I need her to be playful too –
a friend and companion
who wakes up with me every morning
and says, Here we are again.
It's a brand new day.
Let's go!

Inspired by Janet Leahy's poem "Travels with My Muse"

Wonder Woman in the Shower

Pulled in many directions
she has a hard time finding focus
or determining a starting point.
Time gets frizzled away and noble
intentions, sparks of creativity
get lost in the swirl.

What she finds so intriguing is the way
a word will pop into her head
right in the middle of a sentence
or while doing a Sudoku. While ironing. . .
or in the shower.

Ah yes, the shower!
That's where she knows the exhilaration
of creative thought, the Yes-I-Can mindset,
a euphoric sense of oneness with the world.

No task insurmountable.
No problem unsolvable.
And all the lists (the oh-so-many lists)
dissolve. . . .
Just like that.

And she knows she has been blessed
by whatever Creative Genius
has shaped her, made her whole.

In Jean's Garden

[T]here is a time of afternoon, out there in the yard,
an hour that has never been described.

– From "Into the Mystery" by Tony Hoagland

There is a time that comes some days, sits on your shoulder, reminds you, Look. And so you look and see this beautiful backyard garden where all around you plant life thrives and teeny hummingbirds hover above, fluttering their wings. You sit, happy for this chance to talk with your new friend, and you think what a lovely moment this is. You want to hold onto moments like these, stretch them out so they last longer. Too soon it will be time to go – always other things to do. But for this brief time you sit, unrushed, talking to Jean.

When Jean goes inside for tea, you drink in the sweetness of this special place the way the hummingbird drinks in his nectar. You notice green foliage everywhere – and flowers, a profusion of flowers! Jean knows all their names, can point them out, one by one. For you, though, it's enough to take in the brilliant colors, the variety. The wind sways through the backyard garden. Not too hot here in the shade.

After you leave Jean in her garden, you go out walking alone, more aware of all the spectacular summer colors as you get the bloodstream flowing. You remind yourself how important it is to keep the blood moving – no more clogged arteries. You know what it is to cherish what you have, to enjoy each moment as it comes. Better than waiting until the moment has passed, or the loved one is gone.

You consider the poet's words, his reminder that you can always go back to these delicious moments in memory. Like those moments in your friend's garden. Like the hummingbirds, savoring the nectar.

WELCOME

Auntie Ruth's Suitcase

I don't know why I thought of it as "Auntie Ruth's suitcase" because it looked like a plain brown cardboard box. Nothing classy like my aunt, a career woman who worked for Greyhound Bus and who surely would have used something more glamorous in her travels. Not this worn and tattered piece of luggage from my imagination.

All of Auntie Ruth's nieces adored her – my cousins Joanne and Janice, my sisters Arlene and Wanda – and me. She had such a kind smile, a gentle manner, and she seemed perfectly content to be single and independent. She was in her late thirties when she married Joe.

But that's a different story. This one is about me and that imaginary suitcase, clear as could be in my mind's eye when it appeared one day beside my desk, just when I needed it. At the time I was renting a third-floor office overlooking Lake Michigan. I had writing to do, deadlines to meet, and I had to banish the recurring thoughts which danced incessantly inside my head. *Why? Why? Why?* my inner demons demanded, and at unpredictable moments I would find myself bursting into tears. The situation that caused me such grief was one I was powerless to change, but I hadn't yet learned acceptance.

I knew if I could rid myself of those distracting thoughts, I would be able to focus on the task at hand. Sitting at my desk, hands poised over my keyboard, I imagined the "problem," as I thought of it, disappearing into this imaginary suitcase at my side. It was not a conscious decision, not something I had read about in self-help literature, and I didn't even identify the suitcase as one belonging to my aunt. That came later.

What came to me, once I had banished those turbulent thoughts, was a renewed ability to concentrate on my writing. Finally, I could focus.

From that experience I've learned the power of imagery to help me through troubled times. It's a valuable technique even for minor problems. Like the mother who says to her misbehaving child, "I'll deal with you later," it diffuses the present situation.

Most of my problems don't need the space afforded by an adult-sized suitcase. Sometimes just a tiny box is enough. I can write out my problem, tuck it into the box and set it on the corner of my desk, so that I can get back to the task at hand. It's not like sweeping dirt under the carpet, just a matter of not permitting every emotional upset to usurp my time and energy.

I wish I could have shared this story with my dear Aunt Ruth, and she might have laughed at the idea of a ragged brown suitcase being something belonging to her. What's helpful to me now is knowing that the suitcase sits empty in my imagination, always ready to hold any problems, large or small. I can keep the suitcase beside me as I write or carry it with me throughout the day. It's a reminder that, no matter what life brings my way, I'll get through it.

Life's a journey, after all, and Auntie Ruth's suitcase will ease the way.

Do We Measure Up?

From the time we're born, there are people on hand to measure us. *It's a girl!* the birth announcement proclaims. *Seven pounds two ounces. Nineteen inches long.*

Oh my! Everyone says. *Isn't she cute? Looks just like her mother.* (Or her father.) As soon as we enter school, someone wants to test us. Trying to measure our intelligence, our IQ, then separate us into the appropriate learning groups. Fast readers, slow. Whiz at math, not so good. All the way into college and beyond. Take the personality test – find out how well you work with others. Would you be a reliable employee? There are all kinds of ways to take the measure of a man. Or a woman.

The old movie magazines, which I read in my teen years, published the measurements of gorgeous actresses and pin-up models. The hourglass figure – 36-24-36 – was the ideal, as I remember it, and I'd take that cloth measuring tape, put it around my middle, suck in my breath. Never even came close. Trying to measure up, by whatever standards. It's still an affliction for girls growing up. And women too. *Lose ten pounds in two weeks*, the magazine covers shout at us in the supermarket check-out line. *Buy me*, they seem to say, *let me tell you how to downsize – to measure up.*

I have measured out my life in coffee spoons, J. Alfred Prufrock laments in the T.S. Eliot poem.

The persona of the poem is saying that too much of his life has been wasted in conventional living: of entertaining and being entertained in formal parlors.

I'm reminded of a poem, "If I Had My Life To Live Over." In this poem, 85-year-old Nadine Stair lists a dozen things she would do differently: she'd take more chances, have more fun, live in the moment. In the last stanza she concludes, *I would go to more dances,/ I would ride more merry-go-rounds,/ I would pick more daisies.*

During the pandemic people tried to measure the corona virus as it traveled around the world, infecting new victims, threatening our survival. How many people tested positive on any given day? How many recovered? How many died? And all of us worrying about becoming a statistic.

We learned to keep our distance from others. At the doctor's office, the grocery store — just about everywhere. The distance was measured out on the floor: six feet apart.

In 2020, one year after my heart attack, I walk the almost empty halls of St. Luke's Hospital to my scheduled appointment for a nuclear stress test. First, I am given an injection of a radioactive tracer, then told to lie very still under an imaging machine called a gamma camera. It takes pictures of my heart and follows the flow of blood through my veins and arteries, looking for blockages. For twenty minutes I lie motionless on my back, my hands held high over my head. I feel like I am in a space capsule.

Next, I am on the treadmill. Allan and Jennifer regulate the speed and the incline, asking me to let them know if it's very easy (1) or excruciatingly hard (10) or somewhere in between. Six or more electrodes adhering to my chest and back are connected to another 21st century machine which spits out graphs for my cardiologist's review. More measurements.

Some people my age can't manage; then the heart has to be stimulated with drugs. But Allan and Jennifer are pleased with my performance on the treadmill. When Allan takes my blood pressure it's 128 over 62. More measurements. *That's good*, I say, and he silently agrees.

I glance down at the Fitbit I've worn 24/7 since my heart attack, the little device which counts my steps, measures the distance, tells me how many heart beats per minute. When I achieve 10,000 steps a little figure cheers for me. Pleased with Allan's assessment, I hold my Fitbit up to my mouth and talk into it, like a microphone. "Hear that, Fitbit?" I say. "We did good." For today at least, we measure up.

Social Distancing: a farm wife's story

During the long days of the pandemic, I often thought of my mother, Vivian Ellingson Johnson, who spent many hours alone on our little farm in Marquette County, Wisconsin. This was in the 1940s and '50s, before we had TV. Before the telephone. She didn't drive. My father was gone weekdays, working in a Milwaukee foundry at International Harvester in order to feed his family and pay the mortgage on our 100-acre farm.

On days when we four children were in school, Mom's only connection to the outside world was the radio. There was a little Motorola perched on top of our Frigidaire and a wooden cabinet model in the living room where our whole family sometimes gathered for shows like *Dragnet* or *Father Knows Best.* WTMJ came in clearly, bringing Mom such soap opera heroines as Stella Dallas and Belle, whose husband, Lorenzo Jones, suffered amnesia for a whole year. Other daily dramas, like *Search for Tomorrow* and *As the World Turns*, brought a bit of melodrama to her everyday routine on the farm.

And then there were her letters. Lovely letters penned at our kitchen table – a daily ritual. After sealing each letter and affixing it with a three-cent stamp, Mom would walk across the gravel road, put the letters in the mailbox, and raise the little red flag to signal the mail carrier. In this way Mom kept in touch with her mother and two sisters, all three of them in Milwaukee, another sister in Oregon, and many other relatives and friends, most from Wisconsin and Minnesota. Mom was a wonderful letter writer; her grammar and spelling were impeccable. And even though her life was routine and uneventful, she managed to fill those stationery pages with highlights of her simple life.

On the farm she found plenty of things to keep her busy. She liked to sew and always had one or more projects going. She was an excellent baker too. When we came home from school, there was often freshly baked bread, pie, cake, or cookies. And then there were our farm animals: a dog, several cats, chickens, and pigs.

Our nearest neighbors within walking distance were two bachelors – Otto directly east and Edwin southwest, just across the road. Neither had a phone, so when Mom became ill late one night, I remember how my sister Wanda, not yet sixteen, drove to the Schoenfelds' waking Helen and Harold to call Dr. Inman in Montello. He came to our farmhouse that night and diagnosed Mom's pain as gallbladder. Later that year she had surgery, and our aunt Maisie came from Milwaukee to stay with us.

Before we moved away from Milwaukee, Mom had friends and relatives nearby, many of them just walking distance from where we lived. She could also take a bus or streetcar to other places in the city. It couldn't have been easy for her, being alone so much of the time on the farm. But she had a cheerful spirit – wasn't one to complain or feel sorry for herself.

When my life slowed down during the pandemic and we all learned to practice social distancing, I thought frequently of my mother, remembering the isolation she must have felt. She didn't have the way to reach out and connect with people that I had with modern technology: TV, computers, smart phones. She would have loved email, Facebook, and Zoom. Yet without all that, she survived. And we did too.

Stones

A Story of Two Retreats

In August of 1998, I was on a women's retreat near Oshkosh, Wisconsin, when word came that my sister Wanda had died. This was the second day of a four-day silent retreat, and it was right after the evening meal when I heard the phone ring in the outer hall. I thought right away it might be for me. News about Wanda, in hospice care and so close to death there in Albert Lea, Minnesota, where she had lived all her married life. It was no surprise when Sister Marie motioned me aside and told me to call home.

The funeral, my husband said, would be Monday, and so I decided to stay until the retreat ended on Sunday noon. My other sister, Arlene, who had been living with Wanda and her family these final months, helping out however she could, thought I should come to Albert Lea right away. But there was nothing I could do just then, and it felt more important to stay. It was where I needed to be. Arlene didn't understand the importance of retreats, the spiritual strength one can summon up in silence.

And so I remained that weekend, surrounded by the warmth of all those other women – whom I came to regard as my "silent sisters." In their presence and with the spiritual guidance of Sister Marie, I began to reach my own peace with Wanda's death.

Early the next morning I said my private goodbye to Wanda on the shore of Lake Winnebago. I chose a number of stones along the shoreline and arranged them in a way that I found pleasing. Then I added some wildflowers and sat for a while thinking about my older sister who had left us all at age fifty-two: her oldest child, Kendra, making plans for her wedding; her youngest child, Lisa, ready to head off for her first year of college. I offered a prayer for Wanda and her family. And on the several occasions when I've returned to the retreat center, I remember that simple ceremony with stones.

> *Waves splashing over the rocks.*
> *A bird flying overhead.*
> *The sun beginning its ascent.*
> Saying goodbye to Wanda.

My other story about stones is a more jubilant one. It comes from a different retreat – this one in a secular setting among more talkative women who interspersed study with craft sessions and late-night chats. We stayed in a small lodge on the grounds of Green Lake Convention Center. Our theme for the weekend retreat was "letting go" – letting go of all those fears and resentments many of us carry around. Letting go of relationships that had outworn their purpose, bringing us down, draining our emotions. Even if we weren't all dealing with particular problems and problem-people at the time, we all had something we needed to let go of. Something – or someone – that was holding us down, keeping us from becoming the women we were intended to be.

In the central gathering space there was a whole pile of stones available to us. Different sizes, shapes. The idea was to take one and have it represent the person or the problem, the hang-up, that we needed to rid ourselves of. We could paint the stones, write on them – whatever we wished.

After breakfast the last morning of the retreat, we all marched down to the pier and threw those representative rascals far out into the water. I suppose we could have made it into a solemn occasion, accompanied by a prayer or meditative reading, but it had started to rain and so we wasted no time slinging our stones.

Someone captured it on an iPhone video, and it was easy to read the jubilance in our collective spirit.

Whatever Happened to the Baby in the John?

I was visiting my friend Barbara at her lake home in Rhinelander, Wisconsin, when this question came up: "Whatever happened to the baby in the john?" It wasn't the first time I had been asked that same question. Other women in my writing group also wanted to know.

Barbara and I reminisced a bit about that time back in the 70s when we were both stay-at-home moms. And we remembered Viola Wendt, a professor emeritus from Carroll College in Waukesha, who had offered this writing class for women. This was my first writers' group. It was mostly young moms like ourselves plus a few retired women who attended these weekly sessions. We met in the basement biology room surrounded by laboratory equipment and lifelike models of various animals. Most of us were novices and that was the idea – to encourage us to write essays, memoirs, short stories – any kind of prose. No poetry. Vi herself was a published poet who honed her work-in-progress in other groups, but for this class it was strictly prose.

Vi always returned our drafts with lots of mark-ups – she was a stickler for proper grammar and punctuation, having taught English and literature at Carroll for so many years. She had a doctorate degree, so she was officially Dr. Wendt, but in our group, we called her Vi.

Each week we would give Vi a copy of what we planned to read the following week, and we'd file a duplicate copy at the library reserve desk. Everyone was expected to read all the weekly manuscripts at the library before class. I wrote a lot about my parents – they had both died in recent years, and I wrote some nostalgia pieces about childhood memories and growing up on the farm. But then I got tired of reminiscing – there were women a generation older than me who were doing a fine job of that. I thought it would be more interesting to venture into the world of fiction. I started by creating a character portrait gallery. That is, I'd imagine a particular character – perhaps someone I saw at a coffee shop, and I'd invent a backstory for him or her and write a little character sketch. Some of these characters, though, wanted to stretch out of their place in this gallery and launch into a story of their own.

One of the first characters I created was Stuart – oh, how I loved him! He actually got a full-length story that still sits in various versions in paper files somewhere in my basement. Stuart was married to Georgina, a former nun, and he was so, so very happy. He was a lathe operator by day but at night, after their supper meal, Stuart would retreat to his upstairs office in their little bungalow and type out stories. Perhaps he was my alter ego. We both worked on regular typewriters – the kind with the manual carriage return – and the manuscripts rolled out one page at a time. Stuart would send these manuscripts out, hoping every day to receive an acceptance letter in the mail. In my story, titled "Surprise Party," Stuart does receive an acceptance letter, and it happens to be his birthday, but his wife is gone for the day, and he has no one to help him celebrate his good news.

Another story, which was intended to evolve into a novel, was about an unmarried pregnant woman from Minnesota. Her father was a Lutheran minister there, and she was living temporarily in Denver, for the sole purpose of quietly delivering her baby and giving it away. But instead of going to an agency, she left the newborn in the women's room on one of the hospital wards. The readers don't know all that in the beginning chapter though – that's part of the backstory. All they know is that a woman visiting her mother in the hospital walks into the women's restroom – for a cigarette, believe it or not, because in those days you could smoke in hospitals. That's when she discovers the baby, dressed in new infant clothing and carefully wrapped in a blanket, placed right there where someone would certainly discover him. In the last line of the opening chapter the mortified woman shouts, "There's a baby in the ladies' john!"

Well, naturally – you can't blame them – the others in my writing group were curious about that baby – how he got there and what happened next. Though I had worked the story out in my head more or less, I just never finished it. I probably never will. But the mother of that baby, not to mention the baby boy himself and the woman who discovered him – they all have stories to tell.

And then there was that woman I left in the snowbank. And the PETA woman who fell in love with the chinchilla farmer. Also, the piano teacher who fell in love with . . . now I forget who she fell in love with. I have it filed somewhere.

There are all sorts of possibilities for stories if I ever get the motivation to resurrect these lost characters, languishing in my many files. Breathe new life into them. Find out what happens. Take that baby in the john, for example. He'd be over fifty years old now. Hmmm – wonder what he's up to? Today with this DNA testing, he might even have found his birth mom.

The world of fiction – it's always brimming with possibilities. Just like life itself.

Not All Those Who Wander Are Lost

I love walking outdoors, especially in areas where I can enjoy the sights and sounds of nature, far away from highways and crowds. For six years or more before the pandemic, I was part of a group, "Walking in the Woods," led by Dave O'Brien, of Hales Corners, Wisconsin. Each week we would meet at the Community Enrichment Center outside Clement Manor and carpool to a park or other wooded area that Dave had selected for exploration. With Dave always at the lead, we'd explore natural areas around Milwaukee, stopping now and then to take photographs or make a close observation of something which had captured our special attention. Sometimes we climbed over fallen trees or skirted around sodden areas. More than once we reached an impasse and had to turn back. Though Dave never admitted to getting lost, we hikers were sometimes dubious. Maybe we were just "wandering" through the woods. *Not all those who wander are lost.*

My cousin Joanne's husband, Glenn, didn't mind getting lost. Whether he was driving their RV around the country, chauffeuring Joanne up north in the family sedan, or veering off the beaten path on his motorcycle, it was fine with Glenn – more chance to see sights he otherwise would have missed. At an intersection, uncertain whether to turn left or right, he knew that either way would provide interesting scenery. These days GPS can guide us to anywhere on the world map, but such a contrivance would have spoiled Glenn's sense of adventure and discovery that come only when a person dares to venture into uncharted territory. *Not all those who wander are lost.*

Freewriting is my favorite kind of writing. There are other names for it – warm-up drafts, wild writing, stream of consciousness, and Morning Pages. A writer doesn't have to think about spelling or rules of grammar when her mind is in this writing mode; she merely has to let the thoughts come in whatever order they appear and type them out (or write them longhand) as quickly as she is able. Just like Glenn, following his instincts to turn left rather than right, or just like Dave, who would lead us into a tangle of underbrush with the certainty of a leader. I love to let my thoughts off leash, following them wherever they take me.

Sometimes I took those first drafts, with just a bit of editing, to the roundtable critique groups at Redbird Studio and Red Oak Writing. I called them MP's MPs – Marjorie Pagel's Morning Pages. "I'd love to live inside your head sometime, to follow those thoughts around," several of my writing friends would tell me. I continue to be delighted by the twists and turns of thought my freewriting takes me. I've learned there are new discoveries in store for all of us every day. *Not all those who wander are lost.*

It's In Our Blood, You Know

Here's a vivid scene of my father, seated on a chair in our third floor Milwaukee flat. I don't really remember this scene, but my sister Arlene recounted it many times so this memory seems like one of my own. And I *was* there, after all, so it's probably buried in my subconscious. I was only four years old at the time.

My father, Willard Johnson, had just come home from Veterans Hospital where he had been treated for alcoholism. My mother and *her* mother, Grandma Ella Ellingson, had signed the papers to have him committed. Even though he never drank again after that, he and Grandma Ella were never very close. At the time we were renting the apartment from her.

"Kiss your daddy," my mother told the four of us children. Wanda was 9, Arlene 7, our brother Vince, just 3. Arlene recalled that when she kissed our seated father on the cheek, he didn't move. It was like kissing a statue.

There are two drinking-related scenes I do remember from before that date. In one, my parents were grappling overhead with a bottle my father had taken from a kitchen cupboard. I have no recollection of what happened though: did my mother prevail? In the other scene, some men from International Harvester, where my father worked, had come over to our apartment. I'm guessing they were there to offer him rehabilitation for his alcoholism. Whenever he would drink, he had a bleeding ulcer which kept him home from work.

In the years that followed Dad's treatment at the VA Center, no one ever talked much about those earlier days when he was drinking. But neither did anyone try to hide the fact that he was an alcoholic -- the reason he didn't drink. He didn't go to taverns like so many neighboring farmers did, and if there was a party at our house, he just drank soda. No one ever made anything of it. He didn't go to Alcoholics Anonymous – it wasn't so well-known in those days – but he never talked with us kids about his drinking or what it was like for him to give it up. I remember though that he was disdainful of people who spent their time and the family budget at local bars.

I've often thought that the farm was my dad's salvation. It gave him something positive to focus on, and it helped support our family. He wasn't at home in the city; in the country he could be his own boss. And he liked the fresh air, the open space.

Over the years, I've come to hold great admiration and respect for my father. He had strong willpower, and once he made up his mind not to drink again, he just didn't. That's one way to do it; it doesn't work for most people.

I was a sophomore in high school when I learned about alcoholism. Ironically, it was in a social studies class taught by Mr. C, the boys' basketball coach. Everyone seemed to know about Mr. C's drinking problem and the way he'd retreat for a drink and a smoke in the janitor's closet. Not me though. I didn't know about our teacher's habits until much later. What I remember clearly from the lesson in our textbook, though, is thinking *I would never drink alone. I would never hide drinks. If I had a drinking problem, I'd get help right away.*

Little did I know that later in my adult life I would deny the truth about myself for several years before I'd seek the help I needed. *It was in our blood, you know.* That's a quote I picked up somewhere, the quote that prompted me to sit down and write this essay. Yes, there are other alcoholics in our family but it's not my place to name names. Even though alcoholism is recognized as a disease, not unlike diabetes, there's still a stigma attached, even to people like my father and myself, who spent most of our lives in recovery.

There is still misunderstanding about alcoholism, and too many people are embarrassed to seek help. It's not my intention to outline a path to recovery here, but I want to leave readers with assurance there is hope. It starts with a desire to quit drinking, along with complete honesty about the problem, and the willingness to ask for help.

Although my father isn't here to speak for himself, I know he was happy to be sober and free to live with dignity and purpose. For myself, I can only say that sobriety makes every day worth living.

No Uncommon Thing

It's no small thing to be living a simple life here on Scherrei Drive in a neighborhood I settled in over fifty years ago. No small thing to have raised our two kids and launched them into their own adult lives.

It is no small thing – this ordinary life of mine. Ordinary days with extraordinary pleasures. Tuning into the sights, sounds surrounding me right now, right here, in this place. Surrounded by everyday miracles: breathing in and out, whether I'm paying attention or not. My heart beating with a regular rhythm – *tick tick tick*, and all the while the grandfather clock in the hallway sounding out the time in fifteen-minute intervals. It drives my kids crazy when they come home – before bedtime they'll stop the pendulum from swinging, the clock from going about its tick-tock business, the chiming. It doesn't keep me awake though. I find it soothing – a regular chime like that becomes a comfort. Something to depend on. *Tick-tock, chime.*

This ordinary life of mine. In a poem I once wrote, *And all that once seemed commonplace I now regard with reverence.* How true ... these ordinary days slide by one after another, each one bringing its particular delights.

Spring this year arrives in a flourish like the prima donna descending, mere seconds after she steps on stage. Even now I go out for long walks, breathe in the fresh air feel the joy of ordinary movement. Each day, in the quiet that surrounds me, happy memories come flooding back. Memories that keep me company in my old age. I am never alone, what with one thing and another. And when I take time to pause, considering my breath, its movement, *In. . .Out,* I feel connected to a larger, unimaginable spirit world.

Where everything, so I've heard, is one. I repeat those words: *One. At one.* At one within myself. At one outside myself. *Peace.*

Always remembering what the poets teach us:
Pay attention. God is in the details.
In the details of this ordinary life.
It is no uncommon thing.

Wherever You Go, There You Are

I'll always remember the phone conversation I had with our good friend Bob Christensen in the fall of 2020. Five years earlier he and his wife, Charlotte, had sold their home in Hales Corners, Wisconsin, and moved to senior living at the Regency in nearby New Berlin. Bob was approaching age ninety and had become tired of mowing the lawn and doing all the other tasks that come with home ownership. He and Charlotte seemed to like their new apartment well enough, though there was less space in their new living arrangement. The air conditioner was so loud they could hardly hear the TV, and they had to take an elevator down four floors to their car in the underground parking garage. They didn't have enough room to entertain their many friends as Charlotte, always a gourmet cook and superb hostess, had so often done. For the most part, though, they didn't complain.

Wherever you go, there you are. And it's wise to make the best of it.

Shortly before the COVID pandemic put everyone on lockdown, Bob went to the ER where he was admitted to the hospital for treatment of a recurring kidney problem. Afterward, it seemed, he was shuttling back and forth from their apartment to the hospital to the rehabilitation center and back home again. Because of strict visitation rules, Charlotte couldn't visit Bob at the hospital or rehabilitation center, and I couldn't visit her at the Regency. Both of us understood the necessity of these rules; nevertheless, I felt a deep sadness from my powerlessness to reach out to comfort my friend.

The last time Charlotte called 911 it was because Bob had a stroke. A minor stroke, it turned out, but he was back in the rehabilitation center and Charlotte was at the Regency, isolated and alone in their apartment. She and I talked on the phone, as we so often did, and I said, "I'm sure Bob misses you."

"I miss him too," she said, and those were her last words to me. Two days later Bob was released from the rehabilitation center and came back to their apartment. But before she had a chance to call me with her latest news, Charlotte herself suffered a major stroke. Afterward she was unable to speak and unable to hold a phone.

The Christensens' son in Appleton found a care center for his parents. Bob, whose memory was fading, moved in first, and it was a week or so later that Charlotte was transferred from New Berlin to a room adjacent to Bob's. That's the day I called him, our last phone call.

"She sleeps most of the time," Bob told me. Then added, without conviction, "They tell me she's my wife." When I handed the phone to my husband, Jerry, Bob repeated those words to him. "They tell me she's my wife."

I could imagine Bob looking down at Charlotte, the woman with whom he had shared over sixty years, now an inanimate, unresponsive presence lying in a strange bed. In a strange new place. Charlotte was a stranger to

Bob, just as he was becoming a stranger to himself.

Wherever you go, there you are. But you don't always recognize yourself once you get there.

———•———

A few weeks after that telephone conversation, Bob and Charlotte both died, just five days apart. Because of COVID restrictions, there was no funeral. No chance to say goodbye.

Wherever you've gone, dear friends, there you are. I carry you with me, in my heart.

Around the Campfire

My sister Arlene was afraid of handbags. Not the handbags themselves but the process of trying to find things inside of an overlarge purse. In her later years it was one of the things that could provoke a panic attack.

I learned about Arlene's phobia one night when we were sitting around a campfire near Westfield, where we had grown up. It was Memorial Day weekend when many people who had moved away would come back to meet with old friends. One of those old friends, Bob, had moved back permanently. Had built himself a log cabin, and on that night he built a campfire. All of us – six or seven -- were sitting around it, enjoying the fire's warmth, the camaraderie of close friends and family. There's a coziness around a campfire lighting up the night sky, making a person feel safe talking about old memories, feelings, whatever comes to mind.

Bob, our magnanimous host, kept a never-ending supply of keg beer on hand and, though that's not an especially important detail of this story, it should be noted the beer was flowing freely that night and everyone's tongues were a little looser.

My cousin Joanne, seven years older than me, was there with her husband, Glenn. They were recently married and newly in love, holding hands and clinging together like teenagers. Joanne was the first one around the campfire to bring up the subject of phobias. She was afraid of spiders, she freely admitted, but in her first marriage, as her daughters were growing up and the family went camping, she didn't want to pass along her unreasonable fears to the girls. She tried a therapy program to desensitize her fears so that she wouldn't screech or bolt from the camper whenever she saw one. She was afraid of insects and other creepy crawly things too, Joanne said, but those fears weren't full-fledged phobias, as with the spiders.

Others of us seated around the campfire talked a bit then about some of our own fears. I remembered the panic I felt that time I had bravely climbed the ladder perched on top of a raft, with the intention of jumping feet first into the lake twenty feet below. I had to back down the ladder, fearful with every step, as my amused family watched from below.

A few other fears were disclosed: fear of flying, fear of closed-in spaces. Then Joanne remembered one of our favorite aunts, who had developed a whole string of fears at the time she was getting a divorce. She was afraid to drive anymore, so Joanne had taken her to the bank. Only in hindsight did Joanne recognize the warning signs that preceded our aunt's suicide: her paranoia that she was being followed. That her house was bugged and that her estranged husband was spying on her. At the bank our aunt became shaky and confused, trying to transfer money from one account to another. Unable to find her passbook inside her purse, she and Joanne dumped out the contents, our aunt's hands visibly trembling.

That's when Arlene shared her own anxieties with handbags. She couldn't deal with an oversized purse, where something like a set of keys could get lost. The act of reaching into an expansive, secretive space in search of some elusive item would cause her to shake so badly she'd be on the brink of a full-scale panic attack.

I didn't think much about Arlene's self-disclosure at the time, but in the years that followed there were many other things that could trigger her panic attacks. A competent beautician who had owned and managed her own beauty parlor, she lost confidence to cut hair because of shaky spells she couldn't control. The reason she quit going to church, she told me, was that at communion her hands would tremble too much to hold the little cup of wine. By that time she pretty much stayed in the comfort of her own home.

I found this especially sad because in high school Arlene had a bubbly outgoing personality. She was afraid of nothing and no one. As state president of FHA (Future Homemakers of America), she could get up to speak in front of one hundred girls with their mothers and teachers. When she moved to Milwaukee for beauty school, she went into the Holloway House cafeteria and confidently announced to the owner, "I'm here to work for you." (She had misinterpreted a neighbor's offer to put in a recommendation as a done deal and – wouldn't you know it – the owner hired Arlene on the spot.)

I don't know what it is that erodes the happiness and self-confidence of women like Arlene and our aunt. But that night, as we sat around the campfire, we all still felt in control of our own lives; we could safely talk about our fears and phobias. Around the campfire, we could manage.

Glad to be Alive

"Today, I'm alive and this is a good thing."

– Susan Rich, from her poem "Still Life with Ladder"

Some women friends and I were sharing our near-death stories. In my case it was a "widow maker" and I know that my husband, Jerry, is grateful that he isn't the widower. The heart attack was so sneaky, came unannounced to me with maybe a slight twinge in the back, maybe some fullness in the chest or indigestion, though I don't remember a specific call to alarm.

In hindsight I remember being very tired walking into Menards that Saturday morning to buy pumpkins for an intergenerational pumpkin-carving party scheduled for later in the afternoon. It was cold and dreary that day and I didn't really want to go. You know how it is, when you sign up for something or respond with an enthusiastic *Yes!* to an invitation, *Sure we'll be there. It sounds like fun.* But then, when the thermometer plummets and rain clouds hover overhead, the enthusiasm wanes.

"I think I should go to Urgent Care," I told Jerry just as we were ready to leave for the party. I'm not a woman of false alarms, not a woman who complains much about the predictable aches and pains of life, so "urgent care" was all Jerry needed to hear. And so we went. Before walking out the door, I took an aspirin, remembering what I'd read about the silent heart attacks that sneak up on women so quickly, catching them unaware.

After examining me, the doctor on duty said he couldn't be sure it was a heart attack but it would be best if I went directly to the hospital. And by ambulance, just in case – you know – *just in case* there would be some life-threatening incident on the way. By that time, I was feeling fine but took the doctor's advice.

What I remember most about the ambulance ride was lying flat on my back and feeling completely relaxed, chatting with the two competent EMTs in charge. We traveled in non-emergency mode, no sirens or flashing red lights, and they took a longer route. Jerry was already at St. Luke's Hospital when we arrived.

In the ER room I had to lie flat on my back on a narrow examination table, a curtain separating me by several feet from a drug-infused man who had been brought in off the streets. He talked wildly and disrespectfully to the medical personnel, and it seemed to me they were more patient with him than he deserved. I had my cellphone with me so texted my kids and a couple of friends to pass the time. It was two hours later or more before all the tests were completed and I was transferred to a room on the sixth floor with other cardiac patients. I would have a beautiful view of the city, one of the nurses' aides promised me.

By then, that was fine with me. All I wanted was a clean room and a bed a little wider than a gurney, where I could finally sleep. The next morning, I was wheeled to surgery where my newly appointed cardiologist and his team inserted a stent into a major artery.

It still shocks me to think I had a ninety-eight percent blockage.

Today, I'm alive and this is a good thing, the poet Susan Rich wrote. All of us who shared our stories that day know exactly what she means.

Family Secrets

There were some things you just didn't talk about. Not at the time they happened anyway. And not for a long time afterward. When they were "safe" enough in the past and couldn't hurt you, maybe then you could talk about them.

Arlene and I were already mothers of our own growing children, sitting on barstools in the basement recreation room – everyone had those back then, in the 70s. She must have been thirty-five or so, four kids all under sixteen. She could finally talk about it: that time we were still living in Milwaukee and the police came. Arlene would have been eight years old, me five. Mom shooed Vince and me into another room where we couldn't hear, while she and Dad, Arlene, and Wanda talked to the police. All I knew then is that something bad had happened to Arlene back in the alley behind our house, and it had something to do with Wanda.

Afterward, whenever I asked about it, I was told, "Don't ask questions about things that don't concern you." And when I was shushed once too often, I just learned not to ask. Not my business. Or just something shameful, things we didn't talk about. Sex was one thing—anything related to sex, except indirectly, like a girl getting pregnant and then quickly having to get married—or worse—the guy refusing to marry her. Adults didn't talk to us directly about those things, but they weren't so guarded talking about it among themselves. They must have known we kids could overhear.

Or take Uncle Sid's dirty jokes. I would hear him telling jokes that made other people laugh but I couldn't catch on. I just knew by the way Uncle Sid laughed that it had something to do with men and women and what they did together sometimes when we weren't watching. He made it seem dirty, but still, something to laugh about. All the adults laughed along with him, but if I asked what was so funny or, later asked my mom about the joke, I was shushed. Sometimes a look was all it took for me to know: I was too little to understand, I shouldn't ask certain questions. Not my business – go and play with your cousins.

I knew that time in the alley was something even Uncle Sid wouldn't joke about, though. Arlene would clam up if I ever asked about it. Mom and Wanda wouldn't say anything either, so I learned not to ask. And our cousin Janice, who was always close to Arlene, even she knew nothing about the incident.

But that night at the bar in our family rec room, the beer must have loosened Arlene's tongue, because she finally told me about it: how this man, a stranger, came up to her and said, "Your sister wants to talk to you." It would be our sister Wanda, Arlene presumed, and so she went willingly with the man into the alley. But of course, there was no Wanda. There was no one at all. Just this man, with something in his pocket that he wanted Arlene to touch. She thought it might be a gun, but it wasn't a gun.

Somehow, she knew enough to get away and, when she came into the house crying, our parents called the police. Nothing ever came of it; police found no strange man lurking in the alley.

Arlene wasn't hurt, in any physical sense. No one back then would have thought to seek counseling. In our family, it was just one of those things you didn't talk about. Be quiet about it, maybe it will go away.

But then it doesn't. And finally, the story – a part of it anyway – spills out. Thirty years later, Arlene felt safe enough to share this one secret with me, her younger sister. How many other secrets are there, I wondered then.

She's gone now, but I'm still wondering.

Enough

A small gray stone with black lettering
– just big enough to wrap my fingers
'round, to hold in my palm –
reminds me of all I have today:
Enough. It is enough. More than enough.

That word *Enough* printed on the stone
nudges me toward gratitude.
I feel its surface, washed smooth
by many waves, many years. Now comfort
and fullness of life lie in my hand.
Just for this moment – before I go on
to face the tasks of today.
Enough. . . Enough! singing its praises.

Other times, though, on a bleak
sullen day when I find myself
brooding, complaining, whining,
my stone chastises me. Enough of that!
Whatever the task at hand, the burden,
the unfairness of life (reality being what it is)
Enough now! Enough.

Dear Mrs. Griggs

Ione Quinby Griggs
Milwaukee *Journal*
Milwaukee, Wisconsin
February 24, 2018

Dear Mrs. Griggs,

I know you're dead, but I thought I'd write to you anyway. The Milwaukee *Journal*, where you worked for fifty years, no longer exists as such. It merged with the Milwaukee *Sentinel* in 1995 and three years ago it became part of the *USA Today* chain.

But no matter. I doubt if many people today even remember the name *Ione Quinby Griggs, AKA Mrs. Griggs*, advice columnist for the paper from 1934 to 1985. Hard to believe that you kept dispensing your wisdom until the age of 94. You started out on the manual typewriter, graduated to electric and electronic, and even mastered the computer. All while wearing one of those perky little hats that became your trademark signature.

I remember that I never thanked you for one column you wrote back in 1980 or thereabouts. The world had learned that former First Lady Betty Ford had received treatment for alcoholism, and a few years later she started her own treatment center. Elizabeth Taylor was one of the patients there. This public recognition of famous women in recovery provided reassurance to other women struggling with their addictions to know they weren't alone. And maybe they could recognize that they weren't such awful people as they imagined themselves to be.

About this time, Mrs. Griggs, you received letters from many housewives (as we called women at home back then) admitting their own dependence on the bottle. In one of your columns, you gave the name of a woman (Beverly something) – a social worker who was offering free group sessions to women who wanted to explore their own use of alcohol. The word *alcoholic* wasn't mentioned in the column because that would have frightened most women away. Those who were ready to concede could find help at Alcoholics Anonymous. The idea of AA was scary, though, because it implied that once you faced up to your addiction, you'd have to give up drinking altogether. Beverly's group was less threatening: okay, so maybe you had a little "problem" with drinking. Here was a safe place to talk about that and hopefully find a solution.

So, I called up and opted in. It was a fairly long drive from my home to Farwell Avenue on the east side of Milwaukee, but I was ready to see what Beverly had to say. Neither she nor anyone in the group put labels on us – it was our job to decide if we were alcoholics or not and, if so, what to do about it.

What I soon learned is that most of the other participants could recognize their growing dependency on alcohol for what it was: alcoholism, and many were ready to try AA.

Not me. Not yet.

However, I soon became comfortable talking to Beverly. I trusted her – even gave her permission to share observations with my psychologist, Dennis, whom I was seeing at the time. Between the two of them, I soon had to face up to my own reality. I wasn't ready to find my way to an AA meeting though. I chose an outpatient treatment facility at DePaul Hospital (it no longer exists) and long story short, I got the kind of help I needed. Attending AA meetings was one of the requirements, so by the time I set foot into a meeting – led by a kind Jesuit Priest reaching out to help others like himself – I knew this was where I belonged.

That was 37 years ago, and it has made all the difference.

Just thought you'd like to know, Mrs. Griggs. If you're up there in some kind of writers' heaven, pass it along to the other angels.

Sincerely,
Marjorie P.

When I Die

I want to die *in medias res*
— in the middle of things —
enmeshed in the blessings of an ordinary day.

Make it sudden, please, no protracted
illness no deathbed goodbyes.
Just a sweet savoring of the minutes at hand.

Let my life be like Schubert's *Unfinished
Symphony*
all those poems and stories left
dangling, waiting for conclusion.

When I die, let it be on a day I've
gathered the day's mail, fed the birds,
wiped off the kitchen counter.

I might have just finished washing dishes in a
sudsy sink

or talked on the phone to a dear friend, read through
the first two chapters of a really good book.

Oh no, my friends will say, when they learn
of my passing, she seemed in such good health,
such good spirits. A shame she went so sudden.

You tell them then, for me, won't you?
This is just the way she wanted to go
— *in medias res*

Acknowledgements

Heartfelt thanks to my amazing publisher and editor, Christi Craig of Hidden Timber Books, for singling out the pieces included in this collection, and then helping me fine-tune them for publication.

To friend and artist Jean Berens for her sketches and other artwork throughout the book.

To my dear friend Nancy Backes for her assiduous work as copyeditor.

To my much-loved grandson, Matthew Pasersky, for his original artwork on the cover and to Michael Oberheu for cover graphics.

To another cherished friend, Katy Galewski, for my author photo.

To Becky Evans, Doreen Zeller, Mary Jo Balistreri, and Janet Leahy, members of my poetry circle, for their encouragement to publish *Pastiche.*

And to all those people who read various drafts of the poems and prose pieces in this collection, especially: Kim Suhr, Marilyn Taylor, Ronnie Hess, Rochelle Melander, Kathy Collins, Jeannee Sacken. And once more – Nancy Backes.

Marjorie

About the Author

Writing for community newspapers in the 70s and 80s, Marjorie Pagel sharpened her skills on a variety of articles and even a blog ("How the Hub Turns"). She is not an author to be limited by genre, having published poetry, fiction, and essays, and having had six of her one-act plays produced. Her work appears in the commemorative book about the Apostle Islands and the Field Station Calendar.

For over forty years she was a regular participant in Redbird and Red Oak roundtables. She participates regularly in the South Shore Poets and the Woodland Pattern Poetry Marathon. Even while she has led writing classes through several community programs and taught at Concordia University, she sees herself as a perennial student.

If you're looking for a writing group or a writing course, ask Marjorie. She's a member of the Wisconsin Writers Association (WWA) and the Wisconsin Fellowship of Poets, and she has participated in courses and groups that reach from the East Coast to the West and back to the Midwest. She has been published in *Creative Wisconsin* and *The Sun Magazine*, and she writes on her blog, "Meet Me at the Corner." Other books by Marjorie Pagel: *The Romance of Anna Smith and Other Stories* and *Where I'm From: Poems and Stories.*

Travels with My Muse

Janet Leahy

The woman in front of us on the train
is on her cell phone
"all I want is to avoid some shit"
she repeats this in each new conversation
her voice too loud and full of gravel.
      Put that woman in your poem
      my muse whispers
      and use the word shit

We arrive in Chicago,
take a cab to the Drake hotel.
My muse lies on her bed and admonishes me—
      don't write one of those worn-out poems
        she insists,
      make no mention of tonight's full moon,
      no mention of a starlit sky.

During the day we visit the Art Institute.
She twirls through the open spaces of the new
    Modern Wing,
races up and down the glass stairway
and stands mesmerized
at the three-story window that frames
    Millennium Park.

From the top floor she ventures out on the footbridge
spanning street traffic below . . .
> *this must be in your poem* she calls to me,
> *it's like a long arm reaching out*
> *to touch the museum.*

That evening we stroll the Jazz Festival.
The grassy esplanade sprawls with concert lovers,
mellow tones fill the night.
My muse is happy here . . .
as long as I don't mention the luminous sky.

The next day we lunch at the Ritz Carlton.
At a table close by
a couple use sign language.
Their hands move effortlessly in private conversation.
> *Put them in your poem* she exclaims
> *see how words dance*
> *on their fingertips.*

Going home on the train
I ask her to help me write this poem.
> *You can do it* she says—
> *just don't mention the moon.*